A Collection
of
Uplifting Poems

Compiled by Carol Mays

ISBN Number:
978-1537774725

To life's basic joys and wonders
and those who revel in them
(or who would, if they could).

Table of Contents

I

Introduction

As you can readily discern simply by glancing over the poem titles in the Table of Contents, this book is full of beautiful, positive, relaxing, and sometimes magical images. Some poets feel called to address the pain in their own lives and the injustices in the world around them. My artistic vision, instead, has been to keep a sense of innocence and wonder alive and to celebrate the deeper and larger life within and around us. These poems range from fanciful to sublime, simple to sophisticated, and gentle to passionate, but they were all selected to offset the negative images and stress that we are often flooded with on a daily basis.

Many of the poems are mine; a few were originally written as song lyrics by my husband, Gary Blanchard; one was written by a friend, Glenn D'Alessio; and many are in the public domain. I have sorted them by theme, rather than by writer. Some poems incorporate more than one theme, but I have attempted to place them in the chapters which seemed most appropriate.

There is a bibliography in the back of the book, but if you would like more information about the poets themselves, short biographies are easily available through multiple on-line sites.

Here's hoping that you will find something in these pages that nurtures your soul.

Carol Mays

II
Nature

Thanatopsis
(first stanza)

To him who, in the love of nature, holds
Communion with her visible forms, she
  speaks
A various language: for his gayer hours
She has a voice of gladness, and a smile
And eloquence of beauty, and she glides
Into his darker musings with a mild
And healing sympathy, that steals away
Their sharpness, 'ere he is aware.

--William Cullen Bryant

The Flight of the Gulls

Out over the spaces,
The sunny, blue places,
  Of water and sky;
Where day on day merges
  In nights that reel by;
Through calms and through
    surges,
Through storming and lulls,
O, follow,
  Follow,
The flight of the gulls.

With wheeling and reeling,
With skimming and stealing,
  We wing with the wind,
Out over the heaving
Of grey waters, leaving
  The lands far behind,
And dipping ships' hulls.
O, follow,
  Follow,
The flight of the gulls.

Up over the thunder
Of reefs that lie under,
  And dead sailors' graves;
Like snowflakes in summer,
Like blossoms in winter,
  We float on the waves,

And the shore-tide that pulls.
O, follow,
  Follow,
The flight of the gulls.

Would you know the wild vastness
Of the lakes in their fastness,
  Their heaven's blue span;
Then come to this region,
  From the dwellings of man
Leave the life-care behind you,
That nature annuls,
And follow,
  Follow,
The flight of the gulls.

--William Wilfred Campbell

The Coral Grove

Deep in the wave is a coral grove,
Where the purple mullet, and gold-fish rove,
Where the sea-flower spreads its leaves of
  blue,
That never are wet with falling dew,
But in bright and changeful beauty shine,
Far down in the green and glassy brine.
The floor is of sand, like the mountain drift,
And the pearl shells spangle the flinty snow;
From coral rocks the sea plants lift
Their boughs, where the tides and billows
  flow;
The water is calm and still below,
 For the winds and waves are absent there,
And the sands are bright as the stars that
  glow
In the motionless fields of upper air . . .

--James Gates Percival

Night Rain at Kuang-K'ou

The river is clear and calm;
    a fast rain falls in the gorge.
At midnight the cold, splashing sound begins,
    like thousands of pearls spilling onto a
    glass plate, each drop penetrating the bone.

In my dream I scratch my head and get up
    to listen.
I listen and listen, until the dawn.
All my life I have heard rain, and I am an old
    man;
but now for the first time I understand the
    sound of spring rain on the river at night.

--Yang Wan-li
--Translated by Jonathan Chaves

Gypsy-Heart

The April world is misted with emerald and
    gold;
The meadow-larks are calling sweet and
    keen;
Gypsy-heart is up and off for woodland and
    for wold,
Roaming, roaming, roaming through the
    green.
Gypsy-heart, away!
Oh, the wind—the wind and the sun!
Take the blithe adventure of the fugitive
    today;
Youth will soon be done.

From buds that May is kissing there trembles
    forth a soul;
The rosy boughs are whispering the white;
Gypsy-heart is heedless now of thrush and
    oriole,
Dreaming, dreaming, dreaming of delight.
Gypsy-heart, beware!
Oh, the song—the song in the blood!
Magic walks the forest; there's bewitchment
    on the air.
Spring is at the flood.

The wings of June are woven of fragrance
    and of fire;
Heap roses, crimson roses, for her throne.

Gypsy-heart is anguished with tumultuous
    desire,
Seeking, seeking, seeking for its own.
Gypsy-heart, abide!
Oh, the far—the far is the near!

Tis a foolish fable that the universe is wide,
All the world is here.

                        --Katharine Lee Bates

I Wandered Lonely as a Cloud

I wandered lonely as a cloud
That floats on high o'er vales and hills,
When all at once I saw a crowd,
A host, of golden daffodils,
Beside the lake, beneath the trees,
Fluttering and dancing in the breeze.

Continuous as the stars that shine
And twinkle on the milky way,
They stretch'd in never-ending line
Along the margin of a bay;
Ten thousand saw I at a glance
Tossing their heads in sprightly dance.

The waves beside them danced, but they
Out-did the sparkling waves in glee:--
A poet could not but be gay
In such a jocund company!
I gazed—and gazed—but little thought
What wealth the show to me had brought:

For oft, when on my couch I lie
In vacant or in pensive mood,
They flash upon that inward eye
Which is the bliss of solitude;
And then my heart with pleasure fills
And dances with the daffodils.

--William Wordsworth

A Violet for Shiva

In a dim, desolate bog,
between the wavering shadows,
a violet shows its clear blue face
to the wan, desultory sun—
a sweet, pristine reminder
of perennial rotations—
rebirth, dissolution,
waxing from the waning;
all haunting and sublime.

--Carol Mays

Flower Carol
(song lyrics)

Spring has now unwrapped the flowers
Day is fast reviving.
Life in all her growing powers
Toward the light is striving.
Gone the iron touch of cold
Winter time and frost time.
Seedlings working through the mold
Now make up for lost time.

Herb and plant that winter long
Slumbered at their leisure;
Now bestirring green and strong
Find in growth their pleasure.
All the world in beauty fills,
Gold the green enhancing.
Flowers make glee among the hills
And set the meadows dancing.

Through each wonder of fair days
Mother Nature dresses.
Beauty follows all her ways
As the world she blesses.
So as she renews the earth
Artist without rival.
In her grace of glad new birth
We must seek revival. . .

--Translated from the original Latin by
Percy Dearmer and Martin Shaw;
--Third stanza adapted by Gary Blanchard

A Woodland Walk

The pensiveness of the sky
is broken by the cry of a crow,
by trees distilling intimacy
and moist, vibrant expectancy.
Violets, ferns, and birches
share life-giving vapors.
The chalk-bleak horizon
and pungent, poignant odors
whisper sonorous secrets.
The visitor is enveloped
in this pithy, soulful world,
all cells saturated
with a suggestive sustenance.

--Carol Mays

June Afternoon

White wild rose petals
and a blue-black crow
soar with scented breezes
and accent the ambient glow.

Flocking to the feeders are
miniature friends for more—
chipmunks, birds, and squirrels
who reach with beak or paw.

Out crawls a woodchuck,
likely recently born.
He waddles with his siblings
across our sunny lawn.

Sparkling, lacy branches
surround me in green
and hold my focus hostage
in this entrancing scene.

--Carol Mays

The Cataract Isle

I wandered through the ancient wood
That crowns the cataract isle.
I heard the roaring of the flood
And saw its wild, fierce smile.

Through tall tree-tops the sunshine flecked
The huge trunks and the ground,
And the pomp of fullest summer decked
The island all around.

And winding paths led all along
Where friends and lovers strayed,
And voices rose with laugh and song
From sheltered nooks of shade.

Through opening forest vistas whirled
The rapids' foamy flash,
As they boiled along and plunged and swirled,
And neared the last long dash.

I crept to the island's outer verge,
Where the grand, broad river fell,--
Fell sheer down mid foam and surge
In a white and blinding hell.

The steady rainbow gayly shone
Above the precipice,
And the deep low tone of a thunder groan
Rolled up from the drear abyss.

And all the day sprang up the spray
   Where the broad white sheets were poured,
And fell around in a showery play,
   Or upward curled and soared.

And all the night those sheets of white
   Gleamed through the spectral mist,
When o'er the isle the broad moonlight
   The wintry foam-flakes kissed.

Mirrored within my dreamy thought,
   I see it, feel it all,--
That island with sweet visions fraught,
   That awful waterfall.

With sunflecked trees, and birds and flowers,
   The Isle of Life is fair;
But one deep voice thrills through its hours
   One spectral form is there,--

A power no mortal can resist,
   Rolling forever on,--
A floating cloud, a shadowy mist,
   Eternal undertone.

And through the sunny vistas gleam
   The fate, the solemn smile.
Life is Niagara's rushing stream;
   Its dream—that peaceful isle!

        --Christopher Pearse Cranch

To a Cedar

I had nearly forgotten who I was
Until I sensed your easy strength
   and heard the timelessness
   of your years;
Until I caught the sparkle
   of your lacy light
   and showered in your fragrance
Until I recognized your verdancy
   jumping the primal circuit.

--Carol Mays

Rain on the Hill
(from the first stanza)

. . . From the ancient firs
Aroma of balsam drifts,
And the silent places are filled
With elusive odors distilled . . .

--Lucy Maud Montgomery

A Day Off

Let us put awhile away
All the cares of work-a-day,
For a golden time forget,
Task and worry, toil and fret,
Let us take a day to dream
In the meadow by the stream. . .

Where the wild-wood whisper stirs
We may talk with lisping firs,
We may gather honeyed blooms
In the dappled forest glooms,
We may eat of berries red
O'er the emerald upland spread.

We may linger as we will
In the sunset valleys still,
Till the gypsy shadows creep
From the starlit land of sleep,
And the mist of evening gray
Girdles round our pilgrim way.

We may bring to work again
Courage from the tasselled glen,
Bring a strength unfailing won
From the paths of cloud and sun,
And the wholesome zest that springs
From all happy, growing things.

-- Lucy Maud Montgomery

In an Old Town Garden

Shut from the clamor of the street
By an old wall with lichen grown,
It holds apart from jar and fret
A peace and beauty all its own.

The freshness of the springtime rains
And dews of morning linger here;
It holds the glow of summer noons
And ripest twilights of the year.

Above its bloom the evening stars
Look down at closing of the day,
And in its sweet and shady walks
Winds spent with roaming love to stray,

Upgathering to themselves the breath
Of wide-blown roses white and red,
The spice of musk and lavender
Along its winding alleys shed.

Outside are shadeless, troubled streets
And souls that quest for gold and gain,
Lips that have long forgot to smile
And hearts that burn and ache with pain.

But here is all the sweet of dreams,
The grace of prayer, the boon of rest,
The spirit of old songs and loves
Dwells in this garden blossom-blest.

Here would I linger for a space,
And walk herein with memory;
The world will pass me as it may
And hope will minister to me.

--Lucy Maud Montgomery

Hymn to the Night

I heard the trailing garments of the Night
Sweep through her marble halls!
I saw her sable skirts all fringed with light
From the celestial walls!

I felt her presence, by its spell of might,
Stoop o'er me from above;
The calm, majestic presence of the Night,
As of the one I love.

 I heard the sounds of sorrow and delight,
The manifold, soft chimes,
That fill the haunted chambers of the Night,
 Like some old poet's rhymes.

From the cool cisterns of the midnight air
My spirit drank repose;
The fountain of perpetual peace flows
    there,—
From those deep cisterns flows.

O holy Night! from thee I learn to bear
What man has borne before!
Thou layest thy finger on the lips of Care,
And they complain no more.

Peace! Peace! Orestes-like I breathe this
    prayer!
Descend with broad-winged flight,

The welcome, the thrice-prayed for, the most
   fair,
The best-beloved Night!

--Henry Wadsworth Longfellow

Summer in the Mountains

Gently I stir a white feather fan,
With open shirt sitting in a green wood.
I take off my cap and hang it on a jutting
  stone;
A wind from the pine-tree trickles on my
  bare head.

--Li Po

Indian Summer

Along the line of smoky hills
The crimson forest stands,
And all the day the blue jay calls
Throughout the autumn lands.

Now by the brook the maple leans
With all his glory spread,
And all the sumachs on the hills
Have turned their green to red.

Now by great marshes wrapt in mist,
Or past some river's mouth,
Throughout the long, still autumn day
Wild birds are flying south.

--William Wilfred Campbell

The Wheel in September

I've startled a frog, who leaps in flashes.
He and a grasshopper zigzag away.
The lawn whispers mildly, in tune with the sun,
Yet something's amiss--the air is unsettled.
Squirrels and I stash away seeds,
salvaged from spent, rain-ravaged beds.
Bees are now torpid and cling to the mums.
Bedraggled zinnias give up the ghost.

What becomes of the Grim Reaper's harvest,
of creatures who cannot withstand the strain?
The mystery hides in an infinite point—
the one in the center of The Great Hub—
the crux of a myriad transformations.

--Carol Mays

Lake Huron

Miles and miles of lake and forest,
Miles and miles of sky and mist,
Marsh and shoreland where the rushes
Rustle, wind and water kissed;
Where the lake's great face is driving,
Driving, drifting into mist.

Miles and miles of crimson glories,
Autumn's wondrous fires ablaze;
Miles of shoreland red and golden,
Drifting into dream and haze;
Dreaming where the woods and vapors
Melt in myriad misty ways.

Miles and miles of lake and forest,
Miles and miles of sky and mist,
Wild birds calling where the rushes
Rustle, wind and water kissed;
Where the lake's great face is driving,
Driving, drifting into mist.

--William Wilfred Campbell

October-November

Indian-summer-sun
With crimson feathers whips away the mists;
Dives through the filter of trellises
And gilds the silver on the blotched arbor-seats.

Now gold and purple scintillate
On trees that seem dancing
In delirium;
Then the moon
In a mad orange flare
Floods the grape-hung night.

--Hart Crane

A Vagabond Song

There is something in the autumn that is
   native to my blood—
Touch of manner, hint of mood;
And my heart is like a rhyme,
With the yellow and the purple and the
   crimson keeping time.

The scarlet of the maples can shake me like
   a cry
Of bugles going by.
And my lonely spirit thrills
To see the frosty asters like a smoke upon
   the hills.

There is something in October sets the
   gypsy blood astir;
We must rise and follow her,
When from every hill of flame
She calls and calls each vagabond by
   name.

--Bliss Carman

Sitting at Night on the Moon Viewing Terrace

This autumn the days have been hot
but each evening cool weather returns.
The last few nights I have sat outside
until the water clock struck the third watch.

Brisk wind, stars glittering and fading;
floating clouds, welcomed and seen off by the
  moon.
When I pursue happiness I can never find it;
now happiness has come of itself.

--Yang Wan-li
--Translated by Jonathan Chaves

The Divine Origin

All around me November's
Gray, and the sifting of snow,
Voiced by the windy dream
Of lonely Autumnal gust.

But out in its sway I feel
A strong exhilarant mood,
Exquisite, uplifting, divine,
Wafting my spirit out
From those common woes of mankind;
Freeing my earth-clogged soul
From the carking sorrows of life;
And raising me up to a height
Of contemplation and dream,
And a sense, which opens the gates
To some dim glimpse of a world
Greater, more godlike than this
Eternal fever of man.

Ever since I was a child,
I have had for nature a love,
A close and intimate sense
That I was a part of her scheme;
A feeling as of one who dwelt
In a vast, invisible dim,
Eternal temple, whose walls
Were bound by the infinite dream. . .

--William Wilfred Campbell

February Twilight

I stood beside a hill
Smooth with new-laid snow,
A single star looked out
From the cold evening glow.

There was no other creature
That saw what I could see—
I stood and watched the evening star
As long as it watched me.

--Sara Teasdale

Velvet Shoes

Let us walk in the white snow
In a soundless space;
With footsteps quiet and slow,
At a tranquil pace,
Under veils of white lace.

I shall go shod in silk,
And you in wool,
White as a white cow's milk,
More beautiful
Than the breast of a gull.

We shall walk through the still town
In a windless peace;
We shall step upon white down,
Upon silver fleece,
Upon softer than these.

We shall walk in velvet shoes:
Wherever we go
Silence will fall like dews
On white silence below.
We shall walk in the snow.

--Elinor Wylie

III

Connection

Your Eyes

No finer jewels exist on earth
Than your sparkling eyes to me.
Like mirrors set in an infinite row,
Displaying your hopes, thoughts,
    fears, and joys,
They reveal all hopes, thoughts,
    fears, and joys,
Reflecting lights and skies and oceans,
Portals to space, time, and humanity—
To all that really matters.

--Carol Mays

On Wings of Song

On wings of song,
beloved, I carry you away,
away to the plains of the Ganges;
there I know the loveliest spot.

There lies a garden in full bloom
in the quiet moonlight;
the lotus flowers await
their dear sister.

The violets titter and flirt
and look up to the stars;
furtively the roses whisper
fragrant tales into each other's ears.

And skipping by and listening
come the gentle, wise gazelles;
and in the distance ripple
the waves of the holy river.

There we will sink down
under the palm tree,
and drink of love and rest,
and dream blissful dreams.

--Heinrich Heine
--Translated by Philip Miller

Heart of the Sun
(song lyrics)

Images of ages past
coming out of the light—
in my heart
I know the light has come
from the heart of the sun.

Time is a steady flow,
takes us along with it as it goes.
Time has brought us to this place,
filled our longing with a state of grace.
The light that shines is the light of life,
shining out from the soul
The yin and yang—
two hearts beat as one
in the heart of the sun.

Fire and water,
the yang and the yin—
opposites blending, a new life begins,
open and willing to let the light in.

Images of ages past
coming out of the light—
in my heart
I know that you have come
from the heart of the sun.

--Gary Blanchard

Channel

You helped me open the channel
between Earth and Spirit,
revealing my reason for being.

This channel has brought
my spirit to light,
my heart to love,
my thoughts to others.

This channel has connected
me with you in a way
I could never imagine before.

--Gary Blanchard

Two Hearts

Two hearts were called,
Amidst the cacophony of life,
Amidst the fruitfulness of life.
Evolving from timelessness,
Moving in the center of existence.

Now each finds in the calling,
Beyond the restrictions of space,
An ever more central reality,
An ever more expanding reality,
Sensing even through dissonance,
Home, in its ever-pulsing joy.

--Carol Mays

Still Alive
(song lyrics)

I remember just like yesterday, the first time
    that we met.
How the sun shone like a halo in your hair.
We walked along the fairground and I
    handed you a rose,
And I wondered if I really found you there.

I didn't hear a symphony, but a song rose in
    my heart.
I felt like I was walking on the air.
Your words were deep and magical, they
    opened up my soul.
I never felt so warm and so aware.

Time moves on and years go by; so much
    of life has changed,
We travel on but never do arrive.
But through all the years and changes, and
    all that's come and gone,
My love for you is still alive.

As I look into your eyes, the years just melt
    away,
My heart glows like it did so long ago.
A warmth flows through my body and a
    longing fills my soul
For the greatest love a man could ever
    know.

Time moves on and years go by; so much of life
   has changed,
We travel on but never do arrive.
But through all the years and changes, and all
   that's come and gone,
My love for you is still alive.

                    --Gary Blanchard

The Comforter

Bristling yet beguiling winds are
driving snow sheets through the dark,
and, secured by brick and lamp,
I draw a comforter to my breast,
one woven by humanity.

I sense that each quickening gust
is pulling through the loom of time
life's many multi-colored threads.

A hickory brown is borne to me
of ships defying depths and dangers,
carrying dreams and heartaches.

Glistening now—the lucent blue
of fertile, percolating minds,
genome maps and software.

I feel the orange of affection,
hearth and smiles and homecomings,
the warmth of song and story.

The blinking silver of fantasy,
visionaries, piercing sterility—
castles, stars, utopias.

Here is a filament of frothy pink
comedies, dances, and levity,
play and spontaneity.

56

The looming strands of swarthy black
necessities, death, and armies,
relentless in their marching.

The golden promise of sacred texts,
altars, candles, hope,
encoded and translated.

Emerging, the green of recent growth,
rites of spring and passage,
learning and inner progress.

With such a large and lustrous blanket
in which to sink, like a new-born babe,
I'll toss some folds to you, as they will
easily stretch from here to there.

                              --Carol Mays

The Fugitive, #33

My eyes feel the deep peace of this sky, and
There stirs through me what a tree feels
  when it holds out its leaves like cups
  to be filled with sunshine.
A thought rises in my mind, like the warm
  breath from grass in the sun; it mingles
  with the gurgle of lapping water and the
  sigh of weary wind in village lanes,--
The thought that I have lived along with the
  whole life of this world and have given to it
  my own love and sorrows.

--Rabindranath Tagore

In an Old Farmhouse

Outside the afterlight's lucent rose
Is smiting the hills and brimming the valleys,
And shadows are stealing across the snows;
From the mystic gloom of the pineland alleys
. . .

Gather we now round the opulent blaze
With the face that loves and the heart that
   rejoices,
Dream we once more of the old-time days,
Listen once more to the old-time voices!

From the clutch of the cities and paths of the
   sea
We have come again to our own roof-tree,
And forgetting the loves of the stranger lands
We yearn for the clasp of our kindred's
   hands.

There are tales to tell, there are tears to shed,
There are children's flower-faces and
   women's sweet laughter.
There's a chair left vacant for one who is dead
Where the firelight crimsons the ancient
   rafter;

What reck we of the world that waits
With care and clamor beyond our gates,
We, with our own, in this witching light,

Who keep our tryst with the past tonight?
Ho! how the elf-flames laugh in glee!
Closer yet let us draw together,
Holding our revel of memory
In the guiling twilight of winter weather;

Out on the waste the wind is chill,
And the moon swings low o'er the western
  hill,
But old hates die and old loves burn higher
With the wane and flash of the farmhouse
  fire.

--Lucy Maud Montgomery

Canadian Folk Song

The doors are shut, the windows fast;
Outside the gust is driving past,
Outside the shivering ivy clings,
While on the hob the kettle sings.
    Margery, Margery, make the tea,
    Singeth the kettle merrily.

The steams are hushed up where they flowed,
The ponds are frozen along the road,
The cattle are housed in shed and byre,
While singeth the kettle on the fire.
    Margery, Margery, make the tea,
    Singeth the kettle merrily.

The fisherman on the bay in his boat
Shivers and buttons up his coat;
The traveller stops at the tavern door,
And the kettle answers the chimney's roar.
    Margery, Margery, make the tea,
    Singeth the kettle merrily.

The firelight dances upon the wall,
Footsteps are heard in the outer hall;
A kiss and a welcome that fill the room,
And the kettle sings in the glimmer and gloom.
    Margery, Margery, make the tea,
    Singeth the kettle merrily.

--William Wilfred Campbell

Dreamers

Yesterday my son agreed to
Leave his little space warriors
To their respective stations.
I put aside my manuscript
With its struggling words.
We traded in these private worlds
For a trip to a strawberry farm.

Under white clouds flying,
We retrieved our share of sweets.
My sweetie found a misplaced pea
And presented it with a grin.

Here was tomorrow's reverie,
And the magic in it was this,
That two unexpecting dreamers
Found the other in the same scene.

--Carol Mays

Peace Like a River
(song lyrics)

Down through the ages, the river has run;
The river will run evermore.
Through all of life's stages, the river moves
   on;
Flowing to life's golden shore.

Peace like a river flows through my heart,
Opening love's golden gate.
Bringing together those broken apart,
Reaching to those who await.

Peace like a river runs through my soul,
Flowing from morning 'till night,
Causing the broken ones to be whole,
Turning the darkness to light.

Peace like a river runs through the world;
The river brings healing and light.
It flows like a banner that's boldly unfurled;
Let it engulf us tonight.

Down through the ages the river has run;
The river will run evermore.
Through all of life's stages the river moves
   on;
Flowing to life's golden shore.

          --Gary Blanchard

Hands of Time
(song lyrics)

Floating in the wonderland of dreams,
I see the sky below my feet.
Soaring through the world, I see the scenes
Of people living in the world below.
Looking at them, I can see the tears.
And all the hope that lies beneath the fears.

All around me I can hear the sounds
Of nature as she wakens from her sleep.
And behind me I can see the years
That poured around me as I lived my life.
And I surrender to the light
And offer myself to the loving hands;
The hands of time.

--Gary Blanchard

Little Cell

Little Cell! Little Cell! with a heart as
   big as heaven—
Remember that you are but a part!
This great longing in your soul
Is the longing of the whole—
And your work is not done with your
   heart!

Don't imagine, Little Cell,
That the work you do so well
Is the only work the world needs to do!
You are wanted in your place
For the growing of the race,
But the growing does not all depend on
   you!

Little Cell! Little Cell! with a race's
   whole ambition—
Remember there are others growing,
   too!
You've been noble—you've been
   strong—
Rest a while and come along—
Let the world take a turn and carry you!

        --Charlotte Perkins Gilman

Bifocals

Through the window of connectedness,
  the landscape grins.
Introspective roadways?—
  nursery clay.
All the somber mountains—
  props in a play.

--Carol Mays

To See a World
(from *Auguries of Innocence*)

To see a World in a Grain of Sand
And a Heaven in a Wild Flower,
Hold Infinity in the palm of your hand
And Eternity in an hour.

--William Blake

Organic Whole

Our sweet connection to
sunlit forsythias,
leaping squirrels, and
chirping chickadees—
deeper than a lifespan,
closer than a heartbeat.

--Carol Mays

Selection from the Chandogya Upanishad

In the center of the castle of Brahman, our own
    body,
there is a small shrine in the form of a lotus
    flower,
and within can be found a small space.
We should find who dwells there, and we
    should want to know him.

And if anyone asks, "Who is he who dwells in a
    small shrine in the center of the castle of
    Brahman?
Whom should we want to find and to know?"
    we can answer:

"The little space within the heart is as great as
    this vast universe.
The heavens and the earth are there, and the
    sun, and the moon, and the stars;
fire and lightning and winds are there;
    and all that now is and all that is not:
for the whole universe is in Him and He dwells
    within our heart."

--from the Chandogya Upanishad,
--Translated by Juan Mascaro
--Reformatted by Carol Mays

The Deeper Dimension

Beneath the busy theater,
a little trap door,
modest and illusive,
opens to a space
infinite and peaceful—
a broader dimension,
resonant and real—
the silent birthing chamber
of all possibilities,
including, by surprise,
the gears animating
the action on the set.
One may find the door
and bask in this continuum
by stepping out of character
and shrugging off one's script,
releasing and recasting
preconceived props.

--Carol Mays

A Garden Beyond Paradise

Everything you see has its roots
    in the unseen world.
The forms may change,
    yet the essence remains the same.

Every wondrous sight will vanish,
every sweet word will fade.
    But do not be disheartened
The Source they come from is eternal—
growing, branching out,
    giving new life and new joy.

Why do you weep?—
That Source is within you,
 and this whole world
    is springing up from it.

The Source is full,
 its waters are ever-flowing;
    Do not grieve,
    drink your fill!
Don't think it will ever run dry—
This is the endless Ocean! . . .

                    --Jelaluddin Rumi,
            --Edited by Peter Y. Chou

71

October 15, 1991

Scattered images flicker,
    as an evening passes:
Leaves riding the rain,
    in a bittersweet farewell;
A singer's warmth beamed
    to thousands of vehicles;
Ghosts swinging from strings
    in a Halloween display;
Sakharov's casket carried
    in a documentary;
A boy brimming with youth,
    delivering news on
A Union birthing nations,
    eight thousand miles away.

To work-weary eyes,
    strained and myopic,
Just routine impressions
    of another hectic day.
But these are the pulses
    of the unfolding cosmos,
The eddies and streams of
    forces and formations.
Being a mere ripple
    in this dazzling array
Is to be soaked to the core
    with a quintessential gift.

--Carol Mays

The Banquet

Divinity is to me
the connecting link,
the evolution of energy.
and love, likewise,
the dissolution of separation,
the current between gaps,
the transfusion of forces,
creativity unbounded.

Out for a stroll,
I am caught up in
three heavenly visions:
a white cloud passing,
a maple fluttering,
and a hornet exploring.
and these divine voices:
the chirping of a finch,
hammering in a yard,
the sound of someone's stereo.

In one common moment,
I am a communicant
in this feast of life—
its continuing burst
of expressions and ambitions,
its multifaceted forms.
Even the dancing Shiva
does not have the arms
to hold so much dear.

"Brother Sun; Sister Moon,"
This is joy undiluted—
we are each related
right to the core
down to the electrons
whizzing in us all.

--Carol Mays

Gnosis

Thought is deeper than all speech,
  Feeling deeper than all thought;
Souls to souls can never teach
  What unto themselves was taught.

We are spirits clad in veils;
  Man by man was never seen;
All our deep communing fails
  To remove the shadowy screen.

Heart to heart was never known;
  Mind with mind did never meet;
We are columns left alone,
  Of a temple once complete.

Like the stars that gem the sky,
  Far apart, though seeming near,
In our light we scattered lie;
  All is thus but starlight here.

What is social company
  But a babbling summer stream?
What our wise philosophy
  But the glancing of a dream?

Only when the sun of love
  Melts the scattered stars of thought;
Only when we live above
  What the dim-eyed world hath taught;

Only when our souls are fed
   By the Fount which gave them birth,
And by inspiration led,
   Which they never drew from earth,

We like parted drops of rain
   Swelling till they meet and run,
Shall be all absorbed again,
   Melting, flowing into one.

--Christopher Pearse Cranch

In the Beginning . . .

A light has always been glowing
Close to the heart of the universe.
Over the course of time and evolution,
We as mortals have lived in fragile
   transience.
Yet flickering in the soul
Is the sublime, primordial sparkle.
In this ember born of the primal fire,
The transient contains the immortal
And the infinite caresses the finite.
Through the morass of earthly chaos,
The crystal beacon shines, and
Its power has not been extinguished.

--Carol Mays

IV
Fantasy

To Make a Prairie

To make a prairie it takes a clover and one
   bee,
One clover, and a bee,
And revery.
The revery alone will do,
If bees are few.

           --Emily Dickinson

Calderon
(song lyrics)

Through the valley of Calderon,
Past the forest of Koh,
Over the mountains of Avalon,
There is a river that flows.
On the river there is a ship
That travels with the wind as it blows.

The ship sails east in the summer breeze
To the far-away land of Tarway.
The breeze runs free through the spreading tree,
Past the children at play.
The sun shines bright up until the night
Brings a sudden end of the day.

Where is the valley of Calderon?
Where is the forest of Koh?
Where is the place that the ship has gone?
Where is the river that flows?
Where are the children who play all day?
Is it a place that we can go?

Calderon is a state of mind,
Koh a place in the soul.
The river flows through the sands of time
Where all the lost are made whole.
The children play in the magic day
When the bells of peace will be tolled.

                              --Gary Blanchard

A Glimpse

An image comes unbidden
in a quickening flash:
the dark silhouette of
a female, part avian,
upright and still
in a moss-clad marsh,
poised in the luster
of a golden half-sun.
The ongoing joy
of such fleeting thoughts:
a secret skylight
in a 10' by 12' room.

--Carol Mays

Fog

The fog comes
on little cat feet.

It sits looking
over harbor and city
on silent haunches
and then moves on.

--Carl Sandburg

Secrets in a Storm

Secrets sail on the whirling winds,
along with the dark and driven clouds.
Carried aloft with litter and leaves
are invisible, partly submerged longings:

to hitch a ride on the primal rawness,
to abandon all things set and tethered,
to project oneself toward the unknown,
while thriving through the natural chaos.

--Carol Mays

The Lake Isle of Innisfree

I will arise and go now, and go to Innisfree,
And a small cabin build there, of clay and
    wattles made:
Nine bean-rows will I have there, and a hive
    for the honey-bee,
And live alone in the bee-loud glade.

And I shall have some peace there, for
    peace comes dropping slow,
Dropping from the veils of the morning
    to where the cricket sings;
There midnight's all a glimmer, and noon
    a purple glow,
And evening full of the linnet's wings.

I will arise and go now, for always night
    and day
I hear lake water lapping with low sounds
    by the shore;
While I stand on the roadway, or on the
    pavements gray,
I hear it in the deep heart's core.

--William Butler Yeats

Moonlit Night

It seemed as though the heavens
had kissed the earth to silence,
so that, amid glistening flowers,
she must now dream heavenly dreams.

The breeze passed through the fields;
the corn stirred softly;
the forest rustled lightly,
so clear and starry was the night.

And my soul spread
wide its wings;
took flight through the silent land
as though it were flying home.

--Joseph Eichendorff
--Translated by Philip Miller

Night-Flying

I drift aloft with gossamer wings,
slowly slanting toward the moon,
beaming with its nimbus glow.

Like me, it seems to shift positions,
darting between forms and shadows,
darkened slopes and rounded hills.

Shimmering streams grow mute below us,
sending clear, sweet twinkles skyward—
forever gracing souls in flight.

--Carol Mays

Lunar Tune
(song lyrics)

Riding on a shooting star; heading out toward
    a dream,
Tomorrow's even closer than it seems.

Moving through the cloudless sky; heading out
    toward the moon,
I am dancing to the lunar tune.

Life goes by so quickly and time just slips
    away,
But tomorrow brings a brighter day.

Soaring out among the planets, in the vast
    array of space;
I can feel the moon's embrace.

Life goes by so quickly and time just slips
    away,
But tomorrow brings a brighter day.

Riding on a shooting star, heading out toward
    a dream;
Tomorrow's even closer than it seems.

--Gary Blanchard

An Archetype

Somewhere in an old-growth forest,
a woman smoothly moves amidst
shadows of the pines and hardwoods.
Her mossy gown is verdant green,
her hair twinkles with mica, and
her soul, deep as a midnight sky,
with remote star clusters beaming.
She tends the ruins of an ancient inn
and a bed of ferns and roses.
Many a nomad, passing through,
is revived by her grace and goodness.
Though we can't lay hands on her,
she wanders free within our grasp,
For the ancient inn beguiles us still
in the labyrinths of our minds.

--Carol Mays

The Song of the Wandering Aengus

I went out to the hazel wood,
Because a fire was in my head,
And cut and peeled a hazel wand,
And hooked a berry to a thread;
And when white moths were on the wing,
And moth-like stars were flickering out,
I dropped the berry in a stream
And caught a little silver trout.

When I had laid it on the floor
I went to blow the fire a-flame,
But something rustled on the floor,
And someone called me by my name:
It had become a glimmering girl
With apple blossom in her hair
Who called me by my name and ran
And faded through the brightening air.

Though I am old with wandering
Through hollow lands and hilly lands,
I will find out where she has gone,
And kiss her lips and take her hands;
And walk among long dappled grass,
And pluck till time and times are done,
The silver apples of the moon,
The golden apples of the sun.

                    --William Butler Yeats

Fancies

Surely the flowers of a hundred springs
Are simply the souls of beautiful things!

The poppies aflame with gold and red
Were the kisses of lovers in days that are fled.

The purple pansies with dew-drops pearled
Were the rainbow dreams of a youngling world.

The lily, white as a star apart,
Was the first pure prayer of a virgin heart.

The daisies that dance and twinkle so
Were the laughter of children in long ago.

The sweetness of all true friendship yet
Lives in the breath of the mignonette.

To the white narcissus there must belong
The very delight of a maiden's song.

And the rose, all flowers of the earth above,
Was a perfect, rapturous thought of love.

Oh! surely the blossoms of all the springs
Must be the souls of beautiful things.

--Lucy Maud Montgomery

Wild Winged Ones

Sophisticated ladies,
embellished by eons,
illusive, enchanting,
with black velvet "eyes,"
and fringed yellow cloaks,
sparkling with diamonds
at midnight and dawn,
Oh, fly me away from
my grey-flooded days,
from the four-lane race
and the file drawer maze.
Fly me away from
the chain of the clock
and the sink of necessities.
Bring me in spirit
to magical rendezvous,
to dance by the glint
of the moon on the marsh,
hiding from fireflies,
nudging antennas.

--Carol Mays

The Bridal

Last night a pale young Moon was wed
Unto the amorous, eager Sea;
Her maiden veil of mist she wore
His kingly purple vesture, he.

With her a bridal train of stars
Walked sisterly through shadows dim,
And, master minstrel of the world,
The great Wind sang the marriage hymn.

Thus came she down the silent sky
Unto the Sea her faith to plight,
And the grave priest who wedded them
Was ancient, sombre-mantled Night.

--Lucy Maud Montgomery

In Some Woods

Careful not to step
on puffballs and blueberries.
The Indian Pipes are playing
music to the bumble bees delight
as they drink and greet the ghostly pipes.

--Glenn D'Alessio

Fairies

There are fairies at the bottom of our garden!
  It's not so very, very far away;
You pass the gardener's shed and you just
  keep straight ahead—
I do so hope they've really come to stay.
There's a little wood, with moss in it and
  beetles,
And a little stream that quietly runs through;
You wouldn't think they'd dare to come
  merry-making there—
        Well, they do.

There are fairies at the bottom of our garden!
They often have a dance on summer nights;
The butterflies and bees make a lovely little
  breeze,
And the rabbits stand about and hold the
  lights.
Did you know that they could sit upon the
  moonbeams
And pick a little star to make a fan.
And dance away up there in the middle of the
  air?
        Well, they can.

There are fairies at the bottom of our garden!
You cannot think how beautiful they are;
They all stand up and sing when the Fairy
  Queen and King

come gently floating down upon their car.
The King is very proud and *very* handsome;
The Queen—now can you guess who that
   could be
(She's a little girl all day, but at night she
steals away)?
                    Well—it's ME!

                    --Rose Fyleman

The Mermaidens

The little white mermaidens live in the sea,
In a palace of silver and gold;
And their neat little tails are all covered with
  scales,
Most beautiful for to behold.
On wild white horses they ride, they ride,
And in chairs of pink coral they sit;
They swim all the night, with a smile of
  delight,
And never feel tired a bit.

--Laura E. Richards

The Siesta

The sky was yellow, with sparkling beams
in iridescent gold
reflected on the pointed hat
of an elf, two centuries old.

The hostess of the hour was sweet
in a robe of mismatched dyes.
She entertained with merely this—
a kiss in her root beer eyes.

The placemats were of baby fern,
woven in intricate green,
and laughter was heard
like the tinkling of bells
near the banks of an ebony stream.

I boarded a raft for an underground cave,
which was carved in a spiral pattern.
The subterranean symphony hall
was draped in coral satin.

At the end of the course, was a waterslide
in hues of ultraviolet,
with children bouncing up and down.
They prevailed upon me to try it.

Though some might want to interpret this,
myself, I'm in no hurry

to analyze such a sweet retreat
which woke me without a worry.

--Carol Mays

Fantasies

Somewhere,
Music is eternal and dance is the soul
unleashed.
Emanating from bird nests,
Melodies rise with the sun and stars.
Cellos call from sand dunes and seas.

Somewhere,
Sparkling-haired children in yellow silk,
Sprinkled with sun rays,
Dance with no audience on a hill
Amidst the scent of lilacs, earth, and sun.

Somewhere,
Blue, green, and purple mist mingle at evening,
When roses grow without thorns,
And women in glowing robes walk near streams
Of snow landing as natural lace.

--Carol Mays

Stories the Crow Told Me
(song lyrics)

Stories the crow told me, long ago; stories of
    mystery—the only ones he knows—
Stories of history, stories of the past, stories of
    things to come at last.

He told me stories of the days before the dawn
    of man,
When nature lived in harmony and peace—
When all the creatures of the earth could talk
    and understand
And knew that all their blessings would
    increase.

He told me how the dawn of man had
    changed the Tree of Life,
How darkness slowly came upon the land.
He told me of the consequence of war, and
    greed, and strife,
In hopes that I would come to understand.

He told me that the future was still within our
    hands—
How we could work toward a brighter day,
If we can come together and come to
    understand,
That together we can find a better way.

Stories the crow told me long ago; stories of

mystery—the only ones he knows—
Stories of history, stories of the past, stories
of thing to come at last.

--Gary Blanchard

V
Magic

A Toast

To butterflies, bats, and midnight creatures,
To the brilliant, the dark, and things unseen.
To roses, wine, and satin dresses,
To a lucid child-like dream.

To the musty scent of ancient places,
To thoughts distilled on a fragile page,
To open-ended expectations, and
Eccentricities of a secret sage.

To the promise that lies in what is unfinished,
To the charm in the rawness of the fray,
To quests that lead to curious changes,
And rest that unbinds peace and play.

--Carol Mays

Sea Sunset

. . . A city of the Land of Lost Delight,
On seas enchanted,
Presently to be lost in mist moon-white
And music-haunted;
Given but briefly to our raptured vision,
With all its opal towers and shrines elysian.

Had we some mystic boat with pearly oar
And wizard pilot,
To guide us safely by the siren shore
And cloudy islet,
We might embark and reach that shining
portal
Beyond which linger dreams and joys
immortal.

But we may only gaze with longing eyes
On those far, sparkling
Palaces in the fairy-peopled skies,
O'er waters darkling,
Until the winds of night come shoreward
roaming,
And the dim west has only gray and
gloaming.

--Lucy Maud Montgomery

Newport at Night

City lights sparkling,
mirrored in the Bay,
multi-colored jewels—
amber, rose, and green,
crystal, diamond-white—
gracing bridge and buildings—
mansions, pubs, and shops—
fanciful reflections of
countless points of intrigue.
Neurons, lives entwining—
schemes, ideas, and passions—
complex as a motherboard,
vibrant as a heartbeat,
fertile and entrancing,
as though fashioned by a
cosmic magician's spell.

--Carol Mays

The Sea of Sunset

This is the land the sunset washes,
These are the banks of the Yellow Sea;
Where it rose, or whither it rushes,
These are the western mystery!

Night after night her purple traffic
Strews the landing with opal bales;
Merchantmen poise upon horizons,
Dip, and vanish with fairy sails.

-- Emily Dickinson

Meeting at Night

The gray sea and the long black land;
And the yellow half-moon large and low;
And the startled little waves that leap
In fiery ringlets from their sleep,
As I gain the cove with pushing prow,
And quench its speed i' the slushy sand.

Then a mile of warm sea-scented beach;
Three fields to cross till a farm appears;
A tap at the pane, the quick sharp scratch
And blue spurt of a lighted match,
And a voice less loud, through its joys and
    fears,
Than the two hearts beating each to each!

--Robert Browning

Luminescence

Dazzling wind-blown light
sprinkles a wavy surface
with meandering beacons,
offering to the passerby
seeds of sprite-like joy.
The sunlit sparkles shift
according to perspective,
aligning with the angle—
sun to lake to eyes:
Angels in the angles—
a trajectory of dreams.

--Carol Mays

Vapor and Blue

Domed with the azure of heaven,
Floored with a pavement of pearl,
Clothed all about with a brightness
Soft as the eyes of a girl,

Girt with a magical girdle,
Rimmed with a vapor of rest—
These are the inland waters,
These are the lakes of the west.

Voices of slumberous music,
Spirits of mist and of flame,
Moonlit memories left here
By gods who long ago came,

And vanishing left but an echo
In silence of moon-dim caves,
Where haze-wrapt the August night
  slumbers,
Or the wild heart of October raves.

Here where the jewels of nature
Are set in the light of God's smile,
Far from the world's wild throbbing,
I will stay me and rest me awhile.

And store in my heart old music,
Melodies gathered and sung

By the genies of love and of beauty
When the heart of the world was young.

--William Wilfred Campbell

Pandora's Songs

. . . As an immortal nightingale
I sing behind the summer sky
Thro' leaves of starlight gold and pale
That shiver with my melody,
Along the wake of the full-moon
Far on to oceans, and beyond
Where the horizons vanish down
In darkness clear as diamond. . .

--Trumbull Stickney

The Forest Path

Oh, the charm of idle dreaming
Where the dappled shadows dance,
All the leafy aisles are teeming
With the lure of old romance!

Down into the forest dipping,
Deep and deeper as we go,
One might fancy dryads slipping
Where the white-stemmed birches
  grow.

Lurking gnome and freakish fairy
In the fern may peep and hide
Sure their whispers low and airy
Ring us in on every side!

Saw you where the pines are rocking
Nymph's white shoulder as she ran?
Lo, that music faint and mocking,
Is it not a pipe of Pan? . . .

Far and farther as we wander
Sweeter shall our roaming be,
Come, for dim and winsome yonder
Lies the path to Arcady!

--Lucy Maud Montgomery

Bewitching Distant Landscape

The treetops rustle and quiver
as though at this hour
about the ruined walls
the ancient gods were making their rounds.

Here beyond the myrtle trees
in the quiet shimmer of twilight,
what are you telling me, confused as in
    dreams,
fantastic night?

The stars all shine upon me
with the glow of love;
the far horizon speaks ecstatically
as if of great happiness to come.

--Joseph Eichendorff
--Translated by Philip L. Miller

From a Child

Something's wild in the woods tonight—
Something crisp in the breeze.
There's some sweet scent in the shadows.
Hundreds of creatures, hiding out
with eyes and ears wide open.
It seems to me that the forest itself,
young and true, yet ages old,
Is hovering here and everywhere
in a long, black, sparkling cloak.

--Carol Mays

Block Party

Dance, Ladies, dance!—
By the light of lanterns.
Let your red skirts swirl
Like the tops of carousels—
Candy-apple red.

Dance, Children, dance!
With your glowing adornments—
Rainbow blue and green—
Firefly green.

The scent of gardenias
Wafts from urban gardens—
Gardenias and radishes.
The night air breathes magic;
The block has been transformed.

--Carol Mays

An April Night

. . . Down on the marshlands with flicker and
　　glow
Wanders Will-o'-the-Wisp through the night,
Seeking for witch-gold lost long ago
By the glimmer of goblin lantern-light.

The night is a sorceress, dusk-eyed and
　　dear,
Akin to all eerie and elfin things,
Who weaves about us in meadow and mere
The spell of a hundred vanished Springs.

　　　　　　--Lucy Maud Montgomery

October Fest

Homes so recently abandoned
for Sunday swims and picnics
Have become indoor respites
from the restless chill of change.

Secure, still days have vanished
with hazy meadows humming.
Fireflies have met their end,
replaced with jack-o'-lanterns.

Now forewarning breezes,
stealthy, crisp, and vibrant
Pierce preoccupations,
uncovering reckless impulses.

Now uncanny images,
voices of chance and charm,
Bide their ghostly time
to tease mortals hitherto content.

Darts and dashes of circumstance,
figures of flitting moments,
Are creatures mysteriously born,
skipping towards certain death.

So what, if the end is approaching;
the witches' brew is bubbling—
The whispers of all moans and laughs,
the collage of dreams and desires.

Now is the ecstasy of flinging
one's fate to the unrefined choir—
The discordant sounds and initiatives
of many spirits and springs.

Grinning gourds and goblins
bless this annual surprise—
This primal burst of forces
that refuse once more to be quenched.

--Carol Mays

Black Magic

Soft as mist,
slowly advancing
in shadowy silence,
sure-footed, steady, she
searches me with steadfast eyes,
sparked, it seems, by latent lightning,
smoldering still with sultry enchantment,
she stealthily leaps now to my lap, sitting
sweetly, safeguarding unfathomable secrets.

--Carol Mays

A Magical Halloween Pin

As Halloween approached,
a middle-age redhead,
working in a coffee shop,
boldly wore a spider pin.
It had a massive body
of ruby-colored glass,
and was, in subdued lighting,
as striking as her smile.
In that one adornment
of child-like abandon,
she loaned me a key
to a fluid dimension—
a sweet, hidden wellspring,
expansive, when tapped,
of all possibilities,
where young may be old,
and old may be young
where in the mortal struggle
against prosaic prudence
and tired perspectives,
bewitchment can prevail—
a phoenix from ashes—
in magical resiliency,
wondrous, warm, and winking.

--Carol Mays

The Children's Entrance

To children's eyes in mid-December,
a city street winks and twinkles.
The towering collage of lights and patterns
seems majestic and surreal.
Silvers, reds, and living greens
all conjure up exotic scents and
whisper hints of private promises,
smiling, shining, blowing kisses.

--Carol Mays

Flint

An emerald is as green as grass,
　A ruby red as blood;
A sapphire shines as blue as heaven;
　A flint lies in the mud.

A diamond is a brilliant stone,
　To catch the world's desire;
An opal holds a fiery spark;
　But a flint holds fire.

--Christina Rossetti

The Arrow and the Song

I shot an arrow into the air,
It fell to earth, I knew not where;
For, so swiftly it flew, the sight
Could not follow it in its flight.

I breathed a song into the air,
It fell to earth, I knew not where;
For who has sight so keen and strong,
That it can follow the flight of song?

Long, long afterward, in an oak
I found the arrow, still unbroke;
And the song, from beginning to end,
I found again in the heart of a friend.

--Henry Wadsworth Longfellow

Beacons

The eyes of heavenly beacons
Peek out from amidst the shadows,
Like so many playful stars
Behind a mist-blown sky—
Or the diffuse glow of street lamps
Draped with sculpted snow.
From songbirds to sonatas,
From meteors to mantras,
They veil themselves in fetching garb
And wink at us as a lover.

--Carol Mays

VI
Hope

To Mozart

Upon hearing what you heard
And relayed with such devotion,
The soul arises as a bird from a puddle,
Shaking off its present absorptions,
Abandoning its own reflection,
Drawn toward an infinite horizon,
It's nudged along by wind-borne petals,
Entranced by a piercing blue
In a sheer, receptive sky.

--Carol Mays

Epiphany

Some time ago, on a somber day,
I suddenly sensed a channel
through which I could swim to the sea—
the grand, radiant, infinite sea,
promising purpose and pleasure
and brimming with love and life.

Pedestrian pebbles and roiling rain
now threaten to flood the entrance,
eroding this bright epiphany,
but I have mapped the sacred site,
and my fins, stored and suspended,
are starting to bend unbidden.

--Carol Mays

The Bird and the Bell

. . . Waking from sleep, I heard, but knew not
   where,
A bird, that sang alone its early song.
The quick, clear warble leaping through the
   air;—
The voice of spring, that all the winter long
Had slept,—now burst in melodies as strong
And tremulous as Love's first pure delight;—
I could not choose but bless a song so warm
   and bright.

Sweet bird! The fresh, clear sprinkle of thy
   voice
Came quickening all the springs of trust and
   love.
What heart could hear such joy, and not
   rejoice?
Thou blithe remembrancer of field and grove,
Dropping thy fairy flute-notes from above,
Fresh message from the Beauty Infinite
That clasps the world around and fills it with
   delight!

It bore me to the breeze-swept banks of bloom,
To trees and falling waters, and the rush
Of south-winds sifting through the pine-grove's
   gloom;
Home-gardens filled with roses, and the gush
Of insect-trills in grass and roadside bush;

And apple-orchards flushed with blossoms
  sweet;
And all that makes the round of nature most
  complete. . .

--Christopher Pearse Cranch

June

Wild, ecstatic, frivolous roses,
Haphazardly draping in staccato pink
The grassy embankment.
Bubbling, gleeful, like so many corsages
On fresh-faced girls at a
High school prom.
Cheerful, radiant, intricate charms,
Proffering subliminal messages
Of joy and hope rekindled.

--Carol Mays

The Garden in Winter

Frosty-white and cold it lies
Underneath the fretful skies;
Snowflakes flutter where the red
Banners of the poppies spread,
And the drifts are wide and deep
Where the lilies fell asleep.

But the sunsets o'er it throw
Flame-like splendor, lucent glow,
And the moonshine makes it gleam
Like a wonderland of dream,
And the sharp winds all the day
Pipe and whistle shrilly gay.

Safe beneath the snowdrifts lie
Rainbow buds of by-and-by;
In the long, sweet days of spring
Music of bluebells shall ring,
And its faintly golden cup
Many a primrose will hold up.

Though the winds are keen and chill
Roses' hearts are beating still,
And the garden tranquilly
Dreams of happy hours to be—
In the summer days of blue
All its dreamings will come true.

--Lucy Maud Montgomery

Amphibians

When life is losing its meaning,
And the glorious colors grow pale,
And death seems the one destination,
Remember the humble toad,
Doomed to spend drier days
Digging deep in the arid ground,
Seeking survival and shelter,
But to be loving and birthing,
It later returns to the flow
Of a resilient milieu that bestows
The clarity of radiant expanse
And the nudges of buoyant kin.

Perhaps the insular, dreary days
Are partly an illusion
And existence points not to the grave,
But to a metamorphosis,
In which we shed these calloused feet
And bathe in the nurturing nexus
Of our birth-home, the sea.

--Carol Mays

Progressive Rock

On the energy waves of the eons,
Of lyric and line ever-forming,
One is injected, transported,
With all vibrations bursting
Through the human heart and mind,
The jolting edge of innovation
And every positive passion.

Even the cynic or child may sense,
When riding such a current,
The power native to humanity.
Synapses now malfunctioning
Cannot forever thwart their charge.
Mankind has the voltage needed
To mobilize all the connectors.

--Carol Mays

VII

Play

Watching a Village Festival

The village festival is really worth seeing—
mountain farmers praying for a good harvest.

Flute players, drummers burst forth from
   nowhere;
laughing children race after them.
Tiger masks, leopard heads swing from side to
   side.
Country singers village dancers perform for the
   crowd.

I'd rather have one minute of this wild show
than all the nobility of kings and generals.

--Yang Wan-li
--Translated by Jonathan Chaves

At the Library

Pure possibility plays
Among the shorter shelves.
Here can be quickly glanced,
Quite easily, per chance:

Glittering, spinning castles,
With multi-colored shrubs;
Space-suited clowns,
Juggling throwing stars;
A grinning seahorse bobbing
Weightless in thin air;
Alleys winding dark and light,
With neon-green monsters;
Kindly white-haired grandpas,
Speaking distant dialects.

--Carol Mays

Crossways

Summer night pulsing
Streak of jets landing
Sapphire lights winking

Minds ricocheting
Lovers embracing
Cologne, silk caressing

Muscle maneuvering
Luggage uplifting
Strength celebrating

Interstate soaring
Windows, dash, dancing
Jazz and soul rocking

Frequency sampling
Circuits infusing
Earth-force vibrating.

--Carol Mays

A Day

I'll tell you how the sun rose, —
A ribbon at a time.
The steeples swam in amethyst,
The news like squirrels ran.

The hills untied their bonnets,
The bobolinks begun.
Then I said softly to myself,
"That must have been the sun!"

But how he set, I know not.
There seemed a purple stile
Which little yellow boys and girls
Were climbing all the while

Till when they reached the other side,
A dominie in gray
Put gently up the evening bars,
And led the flock away.

--Emily Dickinson

Wynken, Blynken, and Nod

Wynken, Blynken, and Nod one night
   Sailed off in a wooden shoe,—
Sailed on a river of crystal light
   Into a sea of dew.
"Where are you going, and what do you
   wish?"
     The old moon asked the three.
"We have come to fish for the herring-fish
  That live in this beautiful sea;
  Nets of silver and gold have we,"
     Said Wynken,
     Blynken,
     And Nod.

The old moon laughed and sang a song,
   As they rocked in the wooden shoe;
And the wind that sped them all night long
   Ruffled the waves of dew;
The little stars were the herring-fish
   That lived in the beautiful sea.
"Now cast your nets wherever you wish,—
   Never afraid are we!"
   So cried the stars to the fishermen three,
     Wynken,
     Blynken,
     And Nod.

All night long their nets they threw
   To the stars in the twinkling foam,—

Then down from the skies came the wooden
   shoe,
      Bringing the fishermen home:
      'Twas all so pretty a sail, it seemed

As if it could not be;
And some folk thought 'twas a dream they'd
   dreamed
      Of sailing that beautiful sea;
      But I shall name you the fishermen three:
         Wynken,
         Blynken,
         And Nod.

Wynken and Blynken are two little eyes,
   And Nod is a little head,
And the wooden shoe that sailed the skies
   Is a wee one's trundle-bed;
So shut your eyes while Mother sings
   Of wonderful sights that be,
And you shall see the beautiful things
   As you rock in the misty sea
Where the old shoe rocked the fishermen
   three:—
         Wynken,
         Blynken,
         And Nod.
                              --Eugene Field

146

The Pumpkin
(fourth stanza)

. . . Oh, fruit loved of boyhood! the old days
    recalling,
When wood-grapes were purpling and brown
    nuts were falling!
When wild, ugly faces we carved in its skin,
Glaring out through the dark with a candle
    within!
When we laughed round the corn-heap, with
    hearts all in tune,
Our chair a broad pumpkin,—our lantern the
    moon,
Telling tales of the fairy who travelled like
steam,
In a pumpkin-shell coach, with two rats for her
    team! . . .

--John Greenleaf Whittier

147

Trick-or-Treating

The sweet-sour scent of waning hay
    drifts to town from nearby fields,
    pleasing all walkers with an edgy peace.

While autumn gusts enliven shadows,
    the wavering moon turns sheets to ghosts,
    and disguises reveal diverse fancies.

The mind evokes bewitching specters
    cavorting like bats on their nightly hunts,
    quickening the pace of parent and child.

Spooky music beckons from porches,
    conjuring up faux frights and terrors,
    as diffuse mysteries tug at innocence.

--Carol Mays

The Snowbird

Early on a pristine morn
It perched upon a beam
And sang to every school-aged child
The answer to a dream:

"The sunlight skips from yard to yard,
Their borders joined last night.
The snow is draping post and tree;
The air is pure and white.
So come, you lucky children,
 Freedom reigns today.
The spirit of the hour says,
"Let's laugh and slide and play.'"

--Carol Mays

Hidden Worlds

Some things I think are overhead
Are also underneath my bed
And this is true of you, as well.
So mark my words now, as I tell:
Beneath the clothing bins we store,
Under the stairs and basement floor,
Beneath the tracks of snails and slugs,
The homes of chipmunks, moles, and bugs,
Beneath the cracks where waters run
Through garnet and magnesium,
Below the mantle—an iron core,
More mantle, crust, then ocean floor,
With thermal vents, volcanic glint,
Turtles, whales, and tiny shrimp,
Beneath the driving winds and rain,
We find the stratosphere again.
And deeper still, the moon's bright face,
Then stars and wonders strewn through
    space.
So maybe now my claim is clear;
We rest upon a little sphere, and
"Up" and "Down" make sense alone
To Beings who are stuck at home.

--Carol Mays

VIII

Appendices

Cross-Reference for Music

Carol Mays and Gary Blanchard combine their poetry and music in ongoing performances. For a schedule of upcoming events, visit www.celestialdreams.net.

To hear and download Gary's songs, go to the Music page at www.garyblanchard.info. Gary's music may also be accessed via Amazon.com, on the following CD's, by doing a search for the title of the CD:

"Flower Carol" (page 24)--*Stardust and Shadows* CD.

"Heart of the Sun" (page 51)--*Luna Dreams* CD.

"Still Alive" (page 54)--*To a Dreamer* CD.

"Peace Like a River" (page 63)--*Luna Dreams* CD.

"Hands of Time" (page 64)--*Luna Dreams* CD.

"Calderon" (page 82)--*Luna Dreams* CD.

"Lunar Tune" (page 89)--*To a Dreamer* CD.

"Stories the Crow Told Me" (page 102)--*Ghosts of Forests Past* CD.

Per Philip Miller (see Bibliography), three of the poems in this book have been set to classical music, as follows:

"On Wings of Song" (page 50) by Felix Mendelssohn-Bartholdy, Op. 34, no. 2.

"Moonlit Night" (page 87) by Robert Schumann, Op. 39

"Bewitching Distant Landscape" (page 117) by Robert Schumann, Op. 39.

Bibliography

Much of the public domain poetry reprinted in this book was obtained from on-line poetry sites; however, the reader may find the following references helpful.

Campbell, William Wilfred. *William Wilfred Campbell*. Waterloo, Ontario, Canada: Wilfrid Laurier University Press, 1987.

Ferns, John and McCabe, Kevin. *The Poetry of Lucy Maud Montgomery*. Canada: Fitzhenry & Whiteside, 1999

Hollander, John. *American Poetry: The Nineteenth Century*, Volumes 1 and 2. New York, New York: Literary Classics of the United States, Inc., 1993.

Johnson, Thomas, Editor. *The Complete Poems of Emily Dickinson*. Boston, MA: Little, Brown and Company, 1960.

Kilcup, Karen and Sorby, Angela, Editors. *Over the River and Through the Woods; An Anthology of Nineteenth Century American Children's Poetry*. Baltimore, Maryland: The Johns Hopkins University Press, 2014.

Mascaro, Juan. *The Upanishads; Translations from the Sanskrit.* New York, New York: Penguin Putnam, 1965.

Mays, Carol Ann. *Strategies, Poems, and Stories for Holistic Living.* North Charleston, South Carolina: Create Space Independent Publishing Platform, 2010.

Mays, Carol; Bachtold, Richard; and Andersen, Nina. *Mystical Poems by Three Contemporary New England Writers.* North Charleston, South Carolina: Create Space Independent Publishing Platform, 2011.

Mays, Carol. *Poems of Peace and Renewal.* North Charleston, South Carolina: Create Space Independent Publishing Platform, 2012.

Mays, Carol. *Stardust, Shadows, and Secrets.* North Charleston, South Carolina: Create Space Independent Publishing Platform, 2014.

Mays, Carol. *Building a Faith for the Future.* North Charleston, South Carolina: Create Space Independent Publishing Platform, 2016.

Mays, Carol. *Uplifting Poems.* North Charleston, South Carolina: Create Space Independent Publishing Platform, 2016.

Miller, Philip. *The Ring of Words; An Anthology of Song Texts*. New York, New York: W.W. Norton & Company, 1963.

Opie, Iona and Opie, Peter--Editors. *The Oxford Book of Children's Verse*. New York, New York: Oxford University Press, 1973.

Rumi, Jelaluddin. *A Garden Beyond Paradise: The Mystical Poetry of Rumi* (translated by Jonathan Star). New York, New York: Bantam Books, 1992.

Solley, George C. and Steinbaugh, Eric. *Moods of the Sea*. Annapolis, Maryland: Naval Institute Press, 1981.

Tagore, Rabindranath. *The Fugitive*. New York, New York: The MacMillan Company, 1921.

Yang, Wan-li. *Heaven My Blanket, Earth My Pillow* (translated by Jonathan Chaves). New York, New York: Weatherhill, 1975.

Other Books by Carol Mays:

Strategies, Poems, & Stories for Holistic Living—Three genres in one book, on the theme of avoiding some of society's subtle negative influences and living a fulfilling life.

Poems of Peace and Renewal—Poems from various sources on the themes of peace and renewal.

Halloween Stories & Games for Mixed-Age Parties—A short book that includes fanciful Halloween stories, with optional sound effects for audience participation.

Stardust, Shadows, and Secrets—Three genres in one book, on the theme of creating and enjoying intrigue and enchantment in life. It includes essays, poetry, and a novella about a young woman who finds a mysterious carnival in the woods behind her house and, through this discovery, ends up accidentally transforming her hometown.

Building a Faith for the Future—A serious, inspiring book that examines the pros and cons of various religions and some of the cultural factors which inhibit spiritual well-being. It presents a new approach to understanding and living one's faith.

Uplifting Poems—The original version of the present book, printed in a slightly different format.

Carol also collaborated with Richard Bachtold and Nina Andersen on a book entitled:

Mystical Poems by Three Contemporary New England Writers—a beautiful book of inspiring, moving poetry.

The above books are available from well-known, on-line sellers, as well as through local vendors.